RAIDER OF THE LOST ART

THE POEM BOOK

2022
DARK MAN INC.

Cover design by: DEATH

Photos by: DEATH
Design by: DEATH

Guest appearance verse on
"Ghosts from the crypt"
Written by: MASTAMIND

Produced from:
THE FUNERAL SHIP

Produced at: Dark Man Inc. in Clarkston, Michigan and
Walgreens in Grand Blanc, Michigan

Published by:
DARK MAN INC.

RAIDER OF THE LOST ART

CONTENTS

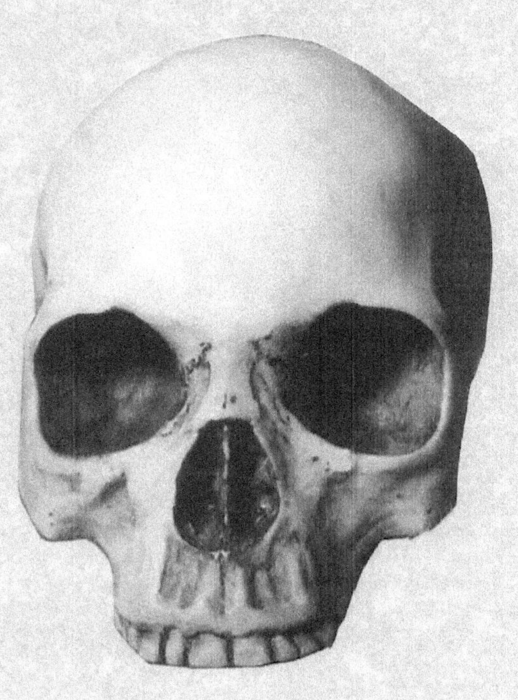

?

All we are; are alone with our own bones,
A loan in our own zone,
Lone we go through the ozone,
Lone one the heaven's hone.

1

Within the pirate ship

Within the pirate ship...
That stole my dead body,
It stows my dead body,
Sole as a dead body,
Soul of a dead body,
Within the pirate ship...

Abode of my dead body,
Bestow a dead body,
Cold is the dead body,
Décor of a dead body,
Erode the dead body,
Froze is the dead body,
Groan with the dead body,
Holds my dead body,
Ingrown with my dead body,
Joy of a dead body,
Know my dead body,
Low with my dead body,
Mourn of my dead body,
No love from my dead body,
Ode of my dead body,
Pose of the dead body,
Quote of a dead body,
Rode my dead body,
Shows my dead body,
Told of a dead body,
Unfold the dead body,
Vow of my dead body,
Woe of my dead body,
eXpose my dead body,
Yoke of the dead body,
Zone of the dead body...

Within the pirate ship...
That stole my dead body,
It stows my dead body,
Sole as a dead body,
Soul of a dead body,
Within the pirate ship...

The pirate

The pirate,
Irate,
I rate with my hate,
Invaded at a high rate,
Evaded their capture,
Escaped disaster,
I made my own rapture,
You made me the cancer,
You gave me no chance to advance,
But I avoided the traps to collapse.

The virus

Sick of their rating,
It's time for my raiding,
The pirate,
The virus,
I raid,
Irate with my tirade,
The raider,
Now I've got them on my radar,
I never was on their radar,
They made my rays dark,
They made my ways dark,
My heart they made dark,
The pirate,
The virus.

The last poet

Carrying the flag,
Strong alone while others lag,
   Ready for the war,
   Battle worn, lone hat I wore,
Heart in art, mourn the ignored.

In the seventh sign of time

The crow flapped by in the rain,
Dark hold that chokes in the reign,
Old skulls exposed in the mud,
Corroded soak in the blood,
Foes froze in the seventh sign,
Erode in the seventh sign,
Disposed in the seventh sign.

The curse 3

Cursed earth at an evil level,
Level never with the good deeds they repel,
Leper to clear truth and the sanity they level,
Level of hell where they revel,
Lever to live evil,
Live lies of the mind through their eye's pupil,
Lip up, angry, curled over gritted teeth like the devil,
Lived evil and you are all now his pupil.

Shilo

Shilo,
My rose,
I hope,
My hope,
Here.

Shilo,
I rose,
I close,
Eyes close,
Mind glows,
Pure.

Shilo,
My zone,
Mind blown,
Mind's hone,
Time flown,
Time so,
Clear.

The funeral ship

Batten down the hatches,
The wind thrashes with wave dashes,
Thunder crashes and lightning flashes,
The tempest advances as it dances,
The gale breeze rips against the masts,
A skull and bones flag still stands, full staff,
Stressed from yet another quest,
Riding in my funeral ship from yet another death,
Tests from yet another debt,
Set where I can never rest,
Tempts me to return to life,
But I'm better off dead, this is my right,
But this is my rite,
Of passage in afterlife, but from left I turned right,
I don't know if I'm still right, so I still write,
Up ahead on my ghost coast,
Starboard where no hope floats,
I see a cruel maelstrom pulling like magnets,
Lure of a whirlpool's stretch to the depths,
Where I'm sucked into the crude, sea vortex,
Reflect on my doom mood on reflex,
I'm spinning, thinking I'm imagining,
My boat transforms into a time machine,
There is nothing else in time matching,
Nightmare of my dream, denying my sheen,
Back to the beginning,
Where my afterlife was a seedling,
Start of the funeral boat launch,
Toast of the funeral boast march...

The original funeral ship hold,
Held in the hull,
My body not full, my soul not whole,
Hole in the hull,
The Dungeon in some insane damned manner,
Stranded in an evaporated lake in the Graveland Manor,
Where it sits so long, it's a crypt of remains,
The Cave is all that remains,
Fades, decays away and crumbles,
The Rubble, humble, but not subtle,
Rebuild a newer ship for a funeral pull,
The King's Chamber of a mausoleum that's mobile,
The coast though, was a lost hope,
The cost though, of a lost cope,
So go reconstruct a new funeral ship,
The Funeral Ship set adrift,
I am stowed aboard this funeral ship,
My pirate ship,
I have got to keep it patched up to keep going,
Afterlife toiling tempting tempest waves on my soul growing, still flowing,
Limbo I am facing, but what is the heat that is chasing?
Is it a welcoming sun blazing or is it a grabbing, fiery, hell vortex awaiting?
I am the curse, cursed to forever coast,
Lost, looking for a hope,
Rendered to ever-cope,
Ghost of my own death I ever-host.

Blood red 3

Yo ho ho,
Bold as I go though,
Blood in a bottle of rum,
Rum red from where it bled from,
Red rum, red rum, murder,
Blood red, red blood inked, read blood murmur,
Murder I wrote,
Red rum from my throat,
Coursed from my weathered veins,
Coarsed like a red rain-stained weather vane,
The world's red reign won't forever stay,
God's read reins will forever splay,
Ready for forever,
Ready for whatever,
Ready to murder the world,
Ready for the bedlam, red rum bottle stirred,
Bold as I go though,
Yo ho ho.

Death IX

The dead man emerging from the casket,
Even after they've latched it,
With the strongest intuition you couldn't even imagine,
Riled rage like that of a mad jinn,
Any wishes I'm dismissing,
Any bliss or loving wish for me is always missing,
Hated, former hero,
It seems that no one here can hear though,
Nothing can stop it,
The prophet,
Ignored without question,
No one would listen,
Prophesying on the world's demise,
Starting your own ends by designs,
Watching you fail following devised defiles from the blind,
I'm undone in a hopeless hunt for a divine mankind,
Where I'm punishing those foes,
Just in judging the droves,
Pointless life of the masses,
Point to the strife that amasses,
Encaged by my own rage,
Pangs of my own stage.

The temple of doom

Invader,
   Dark raider,
   Darth Vader,
Overtaker,
Undertaker,
   Harsh shaper,
   Heart breaker,
Risk taker,
     Raid my own tomb,
       Mood of the insane,
     Made my own gloom,
       Roots where I remain,
     Stay in my own doom,
       Moon on my remains.

The circle cycle of life

Music to make a Muse sick,
    Film covered by a film,
Of the dust and decay in the life we move with,
    Year after year, month after month we fill,
Instilled under purple rain with purple pain,
    Life's stain of strife,
The bruise we hide in our movie of purple reign,
    The circle of life.

The plank

I
BLINDED!
took
BINDED!
a
FORCED!
walk
COERCED!
on
UNSTEADY!
the
LEAP!
plank
DROWNING!

Gold bars

Go into a gold bar,
Goaded to a gold bar,
Goat to a gold bar,
Gored in too by a gold bar,
Bar rod, weapon of gold,
Gold pen that I hold gold in,
Bar with a ban of gold,
Gold jewelry when I'm bold golden,
Bar of wealth and made of gold,
Gold currency that I withhold golden,
Bar within heaven of gold,
Gold place of peace that I behold golden,
Go to the cover of gold,
Goad to the wonder of gold,
Glow to the color of gold,
Gloat to the lover of gold.

Winglessly fly with the vampire bat 2
The vampire bat strikes again

The vampire bat strikes again,
He strikes a gain,
To gain acclaim,
To gain a claim,
Claim a soul,
Name it so, as sole,
So his flight goes solo,
His respect of life erodes so low,
His fangs show and grows slow,
As night shows, the moon hangs low and grows slow,
Wax to a full moon glow read,
His wide eyes glow red,
Biting his fangs within, sunk in,
To draw out blood to drain from within sunken.

Nervous III

The stomach churns and turns,
Like the rings of Saturn,
Outer distractions boil,
Surrounding inner turmoil,
Spinning fuel for fear,
Within this sphere,
Sweat like rain,
Aches and pain,
The lightning inside that drives,
Storms of the mind.

Life III

Raider of the lost art of sense,
Rayed err where I've lost a lot of heart since,
In a world where everybody embodies cents,
All I smell around me is dead body scents,
Because life is just a séance,
Does God see us, or does He just see ants?

Palindrome bedlam

On a pirate ship adrift in an ocean pool,
Loop around vortexes and hex's, trying to retool,
Looter of the soul though, holds the trap,
Part of death's plan to kidnap,
Pan back out panicked, aft a kraken nips,
Spin the ship to drift wave causing tips,
Spit in my face from death when there's morbid even more bad,
Dab wounds with salt, assault to make a whole damned den mad,
Damned by black plague carrying rats,
Starboard attacks from looters with axes and carrying bats,
Stab at me, but I'm on guard and draw,
Ward where we fight to death and not draw,
Ward of a raw war spar,
Raps from cannon balls entrap and by hour mar,
Ram and clang swords in our spat,
Taps, swash buckling, gashed or death by rat,
Tar to keep us in this hull hell pit,
Tip the scales to the debt of death that doesn't remit,
Timer running out and death wants to brag,
Garb of the grym reaper draped on me like a bag,
Gab of storytellers refute me and try to stun,
Nuts because they know I won,
Now death gave me red rum, but I did not sip,
Piston charged my heart when I did not let the ship tip,
Pit of hell pulling or not from demons and fanged bats,
Stab back when I stand tall and stomp all black plague rats,
Star of the murder show, my shoulders hold a ton,
Not one to regret or ever quit, the war I won.

Dark man emblem

A damned man standing in defiance,
A madman in darkness reliance,
Mad hatter looking to right,
Made of matter looking to right,
Made of madder ink ready to write,
Made madder to think ready to right,
Dark man ink,
Dark man brink,
Dark man incorporated,
Dark man in course, core raided,
Man between light and dark,
Man with the rite of dark,
Man within; raider of art.

Still 5

This dead man still tells tales,
    A dead man that tells tales still or animated,
Over the shoulder, still hell tails,
    Tales are forever, still or animated,
Am I at a standstill or can I sustain in animation?
    Dead, but my words and thoughts won't stand still,
I still stand even in suspended animation,
    Dead, but when read I stand still,
A still man is a dead man,
    A bred plan still dwells trails,
Still man then even when in the dead land,
    This dead man still tells tales.

Peace in poetry

Haiku takeover,
Overtake hostility,
Poetry in me.

Curse of the pirate

Take their art,
  Make it my pain,
Take my heart,
  Stain against the pane,
    Make my mark,
      Hope it's not in vain,
    When I mark,
      Straight from my veins,
        Play my part,
          Make my reign,
        Slay apart,
          In the rain,
            The shape I take, irate,
            The pirate.

The eye patch

What you all see IS the mask,
The eye patch,
The black flash with no pizazz,
From my true thoughts it distracts.

To sulk

I want to see skulls,
Rotting bones and empty souls,
Air stench soaked to sulk.

THE CAT

THE CAT

He was a beautiful cat. He had partially white fur and partly black fur. His coat was very shaggy, matching his fluffy tail. One of his ears was bent downward as if broken. What really stood out though, were his bright, blue eyes.

This cat had big, gleaming, shining, crystal-like, sky-blue eyes. The eyes hypnotized with a piercing gaze. His eyes were beautiful yet deadly and they stared with a patient fierceness.

The cat was a loner. He was gruff and straggly, not only from age, but from a rough, outdoor life. He scrounged around from woods to fields, from neighborhood to neighborhood, garbage can to garbage can.

The cat wandered its way to a sprawling, immense mansion. It was large, white and looming alone, tucked away from any other neighborhoods. To the cat though, it was just an enormous structure with possible scraps.

Residing within the mansion was an aging, lonely, bitter man named Glen. He limped around from brittle bones and recent falls. Glen was once a strong and stern man before life tragedies stripped him of happiness, family and love. He was retired and spent much of his time tending his yard. A nurse would periodically check in on him, much to his dismay and annoyance, but was assigned by the hospital.

It was late afternoon. Dusk was settling in with purple and pink skies, laced with grey clouds, making way for the soon approaching night. Glen's eyesight was diminishing more and more as each day came and went. He was just beginning to settle in for the night after a long day of yard work. Just as he began to collapse achily into his favorite reclining chair and exhale the easing breath of a long day, he heard the loud bang and clang of his garbage cans hitting the ground outside his home. Glen slammed his fist on the arm of the chair in irritation and slowly arose to check the noise. He burst out of his backdoor to the sight of his two aluminum garbage cans tipped and spilling out trash. Next to one of these flipped cans was a fluffy, black and white cat. His piercing, orangish-glowing eyes from the back porch light, locked with Glen's eyes. They stared at each other intently, but the cat still munched away on a piece of rancid, rotting meat that Glen had discarded the day before. The cat growled slightly, but did not relinquish his meal as Glen slowly approached. Only when Glen was nearly on top of the cat shooing it away, did it finally and reluctantly scurry away to the nearby woods. Glen only shook his head and swept the scattered debris into the tipped cans. He righted the cans to their proper positions and retired for the night.

The cat began to visit Glen during the day as he worked in the yard. The cat would watch patiently and intently from a distance as Glen tended to his yard. This happened day in and day out for weeks and the cat would inch in closer and closer each time.

One day while Glen was bent over weeding out his garden in the backyard, he felt a slight nudge and rub against his leg. He was a little alarmed, but eased when he noticed it was the furry feline rubbing against him that had been frequenting his yard as of late. Glen began to pet and greet the animal in loving and fascinated amazement.

On Glen's next nurse visit, he instructed her to start bringing him cat food. She reluctantly obliged for she was in fact not a fan of cats. She absolutely did not trust these creatures. She was highly annoyed at the prospect of Glen feeding a stray animal, especially a cat at that.

Glen began to routinely feed the cat every day and every night. The cat became something to which Glen could look forward to each day and fill his void of loneliness. Eventually, Glen began letting the cat into his home, essentially adopting it as a pet.

Glen's new pet was much to the dismay of his nurse, who truly hated cats. At her own home, stray cats were not only shooed away forcefully, but some were hurt and poisoned to death. So, she was not happy with the presence of her client's new pet to say the least.

Glen not so cleverly named the cat, Cat. Glen loved and cared for the cat very much. He trusted, befriended, confided and cried to the cat. He routinely fed his pet and petted him often. The cat even eventually began to sit and settle on Glen's lap every night when he relaxed in his chair to watch television.

The nurse and the cat were not getting along at all. The cat often appeared out-of-nowhere and startled the nurse. She would gasp with fright every time and the cat would growl deeply within its throat while his bright, blue eyes glowed profusely.

The nurse expressed her concerns to Glen about the cat on many occasions. She claimed that the cat gave her an eerie feeling and she was convinced it had an aura of evil about him. Glen only dismissed her claims as nonsense.

The cat began to dart out in front of the nurse whenever she walked by him. He would quickly weave through her moving feet, nearly tripping her each time. She would yell out in frightful rage and curse at the cat.

The nurse was getting aggravated and very leery of the cat. Dread began to fill her whenever the days would come for her to check on and tend to Glen. She felt as if the cat was out to get her.

It was to be the nurse's final visit to Glen. She told him a phony excuse that she was leaving the business of caretaking. The truth though, was that the nurse was sick of being scared out of her wits from the cat lurking around every corner and the often-perceived tripping attempts. Her plan was to poison the cat's food before she left for good.

To Glen's surprise, the nurse insisted on feeding the cat before she left. He allowed it, thinking that would be her last good deed before leaving. She secretly prepared the meal while Glen did some yard work. She carefully mixed the poison in as she scraped the wet cat food from the can and onto a small saucer. She easingly made kissing and clicking sounds with her mouth to call the cat out for lunch. She tapped the side of the plate with a fork while she walked with it, calling the cat. She peered around with plate in hand impatiently waiting for the cat. Suddenly, the cat burst from out-of-nowhere and darted between her feet as she stalked. The nurse let out a brief screech as she went crashing to the ground from the cat's trip. The saucer cracked and shattered on the floor as she fell. During her descent to the linoleum-tiled floor, her head smacked against the corner of the counter top. Her head's popping bump only slightly slowed the heavy fall to the ground. The cat stared intently, growling with orange-glowing eyes as the nurse kicked and convulsed on the floor in a bloody heap.

Glen heard the scream and loud thud from outside and quickly ran in to see what was the matter. He was shocked to see the nurse in a pool of blood with the cat hunched calmly nearby, watching. Glen frantically called 911, but by time the medic's arrived it was too late. The nurse was dead.

Glen pondered on what could have happened for many days. He could not believe it and was eventually convinced that it was not an accident as officials had claimed. Past conversations with the nurse kept replaying within his mind. He was sure that the cat had caused this death.

The cat had a knack for sensing energy. He had a strong intuition and could feel moods. He could sense hatred and anger. It was almost certain that he sensed the nurse's deep disdain for him. So it would stand to reason, that he would then feel the vibes emanating from Glen as well.

Glen wanted to be rid of the cat. His plan was to capture the cat and either have him put down or dropped into the woods somewhere far off. The cat seemed to be hiding from Glen though. He would not even emerge for feedings any longer. Glen would only catch brief glimpses of the cat scurrying around corners of the house. Glen often felt like he was being watched and on many occasions even stalked, like prey. He could not shake this feeling that dreaded him.

Glen was set for a replacement nurse to arrive the following day. Of course, his first conversation with her would be warnings of the cat. So, Glen was spending the day getting the house in order and setting a live trap for a chance capture of the roaming cat.

Glen had just heated himself up a t.v. dinner in the microwave to eat. He was carrying it to his trusty, reclining chair for dinner, television and relaxation for the night. The cat had other plans. As Glen slowly walked across the kitchen with his hot tray, the cat darted out in front of him, sliding between his feet and purposely tripping him. Glen's meal flew and splattered across the kitchen floor. He quickly collapsed, banging his head on the edge of the counter top in much the same way as the nurse did. In Glen's case though, his neck was kinked and wrenched in a horrific manner against the counter and lower cupboards. Glen was knocked unconscious immediately upon impact. The cat just sat by and cleaned himself in triumphant, purring calmness.

The following morning, the new nurse arrived to begin her duties with Glen. After a series of knocks on the door with no answer, the nurse carefully let herself into the house. She called Glen's name aloud multiple times as she entered. As the nurse cautiously crept through the house calling out, she began to hear a groaning sound coming from the kitchen. When she went into the kitchen, she witnessed Glen laying on the floor with his head and neck bent awkwardly against the cupboard. He was blinking rapidly, groaning and breathing laboriously. The nurse proceeded to call an ambulance, which promptly arrived to take Glen away and care for him at the hospital. The cat was nowhere to be found.

Glen's diagnosis was not good. It was found that because of his fall, Glen would permanently be paralyzed from the neck down. Glen would need more care than ever before. His new nurse stayed and moved into a spare bedroom. She had been preparing his home for his new life challenges.

The knock to Glen's head rendered him a bit incoherent and often hard to understand. So, when he began to panic upon hearing the news that he was coming back home, babbling about the murderous cat, he was dismissed as paranoid and insane.

Upon returning home, Glen was greeted heartily by his new nurse. He was immediately mumbling with paranoia about the cat. The nurse just tried to shush him easingly as he was wheeled into his bedroom. The nurse to that point still had not even laid eyes on this mysterious cat. She actually assumed and concluded that Glen was mistaken with paranoid delusion and there was no cat. The nurse insistently gave him a sedative to calm and allow rest.

It was a cold, dark, stormy night. Glen snoozed restlessly as lightning flared and flashed brightly across his dark bedroom. The nurse snored undisturbed down the hall in her room. Glen was startled from his slumber frequently as the thunder crashed and banged about. In the various lightning blasts of light, he spotted a creeping cat shadow. With each spark of bright spotlight, the shadow crept ever closer. Glen attempted to scream out, but his throat was too dry and hoarse.

The cat jumped up onto Glen's bed, deeply growling and frightening him to the core. It had orange-tinted, glowing, fiery eyes. Glen could not feel the cat's weight because of his paralysis nor could he move. The cat just stared with blazing eyes and Glen was still unable to yell out.

The cat slowly and carefully began to crawl up the sheets toward Glen's face. Glen's mouth was agape as if to scream aloud, but no sound would come out. While his mouth was frozen open with terror, the cat dove. Its sharp, hooked claws latched into Glen's tongue, while its fangs clamped and chomped in. The cat ripped and severed Glen's tongue completely from his mouth. Glen could only mumble muffled screeches through gurgled blood. The cat chewed the gum-like, pink tongue and consumed it entirely as he eyed more of Glen's face. Glen painfully shook his head the best he could, but the cat dug its nails in his cheeks fiercely and ferociously to hold his head steady. The next course in the cat's merciless meal was Glen's nose. The cat munched and gnawed away at the chewy, protruding nose through Glen's stifled cries. Glen moaned in painful, helpless despair as the cat maintained its grip and inched a little higher up his face. Glen tried to blink rapidly to stop the attack, but the cat snatched his eyelids with its sharp teeth and tore them each off with a snap. Glen cried out coarsely, but to no avail. The cat bit into Glen's gooey eyeball glob. He could feel the cat snorting heavy breath onto his face as it munched into the marshmallow-like, dripping gob. The cat growled lowly and deeply while it ate Glen's eyes. Glen was nearly unconscious at this point as the cat loosened its grip on his face. The cat then loomed over Glen's neck and his throat looked to be the entrée. The cat sunk its razor teeth in, causing blood to ooze out in a pool. The cat chewed and crunched into the Adam's apple as Glen gurgled his final breaths. The cat carved out a hallowed out niche in Glen's throat and neck. The sheets were drenched with Glen's urine and sweat. His pillow was dampened with blood. The cat sat on Glen contently and cleaned itself, licking its paws and face of blood for a few moments.

In the morning the nurse discovered the macabre horror, greeted with shrieks of disbelief. Through her tears and shocked sobs, she saw bloody paw prints leading from the body and out of the window.

Ghost writer 3

The ghost rider,
The ghost right here,
Ghost righter,
The ghost rights errs,
The ghost radar,
Ghost raider,
The ghost rite hour,
Ghost writer.

Ghosts from the crypt

Mike
The cemetery fog lifts in mystic mist,
   Arose dew that moves across a full moon,
   Where gloom looms and weak souls swoon,
Naked trees shedding leaves in this midst,
Pieces amiss, solace quits when it's missed,
   Peace is adrift, when ghouls drift with cold moods,
   Cracked tombstones and crooked crosses that hold doom,
A house to haunt with all that it admits,
      Admission of the spirits who won't rest in peace,
         Pieces of bones and skulls on the mantle,
      Mission of specters who won't be appeased,
         Flames flicker on candles,
      Restless cobwebs sway with the breath or breeze,
         Ghosts from corroded coffins with rusted handles.

Mastamind
The souls of the lost walk dark pathways,
   The search for clarity never ends,
   The daily chore of cleansing all sins,
   When does the forgiveness begin,
   Tears dry by the wind,
Escaping hellfire only halfway,
Bones melt away but spirits never decay,
      Naked trees shedding leaves in the cold breeze,
         Ashes to ashes dust to dust,
         Undying souls never exit in such a rush,
            Spirits too alive to concede to the darkness of night,
            Rather feel the pain of a rusty knife,
            A never-ending lust for life,
               Wet soil weighs down the coffin deep underground,
               Souls cry out as only angels hear the sweet sound.

My poems

My poems all along have been one long suicide note,
My poems all along have been one long homicide of hope,
My poems have all along been...

My own Antidote,
Spoke from a funeral Boat,
The way that I Cope,
My own special Dose,
Where I Evoke,
Where my thoughts Float,
Memories of a Ghost,
Where I can be the Host,
My will Imposed,
A frown to a Joke,
Where I just Know,
Where I'm just Low,
A hope to host with the Most,
One long confession Note,
My own Odes,
My own words Posed,
My own Quotes,
The voice of my corpse hung from a Rope,
Where my pain Soaks,
Where my brain is Transposed,
Where my veins are Unfroze,
My own misanthrope Vote,
Where my feelings are Wrote,
Where I'm eXposed,
Where my mind and pen are Yoked,
Where I'm more than Zeroed.

My poems all along have been one long suicide note,
My poems all along have been one long homicide of hope.

The last crusade

The last crusade,
    The last time for pain,
Let the rain cascade,
    Until I take the reins.

The kraken

What would happen
If you happen upon a kraken?
With long tentacles it is fashioned,
Go fasten the hatches you batten!

Could the ship still sail cast winds
If it was crashed in by the kraken?
It has suction cups attached on,
Seal fast and hasten, don't let a crack in!

Could the ship remain captained
If it was collapsed in by the kraken?
It is bigger than ever imagined,
Hold fast so the ship won't then crack in!

Could the ship stay masted
If it was snapped in half by the kraken?
Its large beak smacked in,
Deal fast, you can't last in the smash in!

Death's blast VI Set my own trap

Still in the mainstream world's trap,
Part of some insane dream, constructed to strap,
Parts my heart while I lay in my coffin and nap,
Pan out to the overview and on the lid they rap,
Par with wicked plans as they tap,
Pat and stand pat as they awake me with a slap,
Pals never, woke and weak they wake my sleep with a snap,
Pans of worldly, fake news, with hate views they wield and yap,
Pay them back with the vampire black bat and fanged black cat that wait on my lap,
Pal and familiar sit, set with my own trap.

Captain Hook

Angle hook that dangles,
　　Lure of allure,
　　　Snatch of the pussycat,
　　Lure of a lure,
　　　　Snag it up, never get enough,
　　　　　Hooked,
　　　　　　Good mood or groom doom,
　　　　　Pleasure hook,
　　　　　Treasure hook,
　　　　　Hooked.

Angled hook that strangles,
　　Hurts and herds,
　　　Scratch of aristocrats,
　　Worth damned worse,
　　　　Lacked with love, never given up,
　　　　　Hooked,
　　　　　　Trued tune or mood doomed,
　　　　　Provoking hook,
　　　　　Choking hook,
　　　　　Hooked.

Wrangled hook that mangles,
　　Murder the deserved,
　　　Wrath of the psychopath,
　　Blur of the cursed,
　　　　Dragged in blood, never settled grudge,
　　　　　Hooked,
　　　　　　Assume doom or doom ensues,
　　　　　Revenge hook,
　　　　　Avenge hook,
　　　　　Hooked.

The parrot

What becomes of the parrot?
The story is sad, it's apparent,
Once so beautiful and colorful,
Danced and sung, so wonderful and loveable,
The mirage is now a popped bubble,
After a life of much struggle,
Now she is straggly, scabbed, scarred and stressed,
Feathers falling out and messed,
Watching my favorite bird sink,
Tweaks, stinks, her mind's on the brink,
Defeated and weak, she can't think,
Blindly sees things, she thinks,
Wreaks havoc when she seeks,
Where paranoia seeps,
Allusive when she speaks,
Intrusive with her beak,
She once sat upon my shoulder,
A good girl and petted lover,
Now she more resembles a vulture,
Lurking cruelly over my shoulder to torture,
Always imploring, insulting and inquiring,
Staring with destructive desiring,
Eyes once inviting and admiring,
Are now wide and psychotic with miring,
She squawks and talks nonstop,
Spoken nonsense, ridiculousness that don't stop,
Speaking so many lies that her tongue is rotting out,
Venom dripping from her rotting mouth,
She constantly annoyed and felt paranoid,
Her life was left destroyed,
In my life she left a void,
The end she can't avoid.

Black heart the pirate

My black heart is from lacked love,
It is filled with black blood,
I could lash out with a black tongue,
Instead I write; rite of the masked one,
Love given, but none received,
Blood given, bloodletting, my eyes bleed,
From what my eyes see,
Raider of the lost art that I seize.

Skeleton key

See through the key hole,
But see the map key whole,
Knowledge is key,
But God has the key,
God is the key,
He is always on key,
The keynote teacher,
The keynote speaker.

Dead man's chest

Dead man's chest,
Dread man's death,
Strong bound locks,
Oblong box,
Latched in meal,
Casket sealed,
Coffin interment,
Often inter meant,
Bound in a hold,
Down in a hole,
Laid in graveyard,
Paid some grave charge,
Enlightened cemetery,
End life in symmetry,
Be low amid moods honed,
Below a grim tombstone,
Heads low, hung above,
Headstone up above,
Potted and zoned ardent,
Pod in a stone garden,
A rest in tomb,
Arrested loom,
Hail from the crypt,
Tale from the crypt,
Drawn cursed batch,
Long dirt nap,
Bed in depths,
Dead man's chest.

The cask of McCluskey

What is dark if there is no light left?
The light left,
Ignite death,
The night's guest,
I might guess,
My might's test,
Temptingness step to fight breath,
No rights left,
The rites crept,
Crypt where my sight's kept,
I couldn't see the sunlight less,
Freedom in a closed tight chest,
Sarcophagus for right rest.

The moods of time

Faith is wading, waiting, faith is patience,
  When it's agonizing, patience is death,
Fate integrated in an inpatient,
  When they're analyzed, the patients in depth,
    Sown to expose the real life in the light,
      Show shown under the shone light of the moon,
    Thrown to a throne, enlightened in insight,
      Though to go glow, ignited through the gloom,
        So who would mind, who does mind, who can mind?
          Go and go, always goes, who can tell time?
        Sow, it's dug like a mine, the doom of mind,
          Slow or fast, change pasts, passed the moods of time,
            Eluded the illusions sent from God,
            Diluted tools alluded to by God.

The buried treasure

The buried treasure,
    Within a chest,
Dig for pleasure,
    The rewards are best,
      It is a heart,
        Beware the curse,
      Don't rip it apart,
        The hurt is worst.

Dedication to poetry

Destroy,
Enjoy,
Rite to reinvent,
Some more ways for me to vent,
Write to represent.

The poet

The unimportant,
The poet,
Writing lunatic.

A life buried alive

Down in a pit,
Dirt ready to tip,
Cover me from the top,
I feel like a seed in a pot,
I feel the dread in my gut,
I feel the afterlife tug,
Waiting for me to depart to the deep part,
Hole of a deep trap,
The whole thing seems evil,
So, how can I live?
Will anyone save me from this spot?
But my tombstone, it already tops.

A leaf

The tumbling leaf leaves,
Nature's course leaves leaves,
Leaves all leave,
Leaves alleve,
From right to left leaf,
A left leaf,
From rights to death leaf,
A left leaf,
From rite to swept leaf,
A left leaf,
A leave,
A leaf.

Trying time

Try to write happy,
　Rhyme glad when I'm sad,
Die to write crafty,
　In my hands when it's bad,
　　Had to try,
　　　When they deny my brand,
　　Hang me high,
　　　When they despise my stand,
　　　　Damned in a curse,
　　　　　Hurt me as a man,
　　　　Ran to the hearse,
　　　　　Stir me because they can,
　　　　　　Worthy when I'm trying time,
　　　　　　Unworthy in their trying times.

The crystal skull

I am the crystal skull,
Thirteen souls afflict my skull,
Thirteen mimes that lift and cull,
My skull glows when the moon is mystical full,
And theirs glow green with orange eyes,
Faces of death with a spiritual core rise,
See through their eyes, through your eyes they greeted,
Beat it or be defeated.

DEATH in my crystal skull,
Debt magnet that sticks and pulls,
PAIN in my crystal skull,
Pane to show that grit is full,
FEAR in my crystal skull,
Fee here that grows you invincible,
INSANITY in my crystal skull,
Ends sanity if it's plentiful,
EVIL in my crystal skull,
Evolve when it grips and stalls,
HATE in my crystal skull,
Height that within lives a bull,
RAGE in my crystal skull,
Range that explodes powerful,
WORRY in my crystal skull,
Warring that grows pitiful,
FATE in my crystal skull,
Fades or grows, amiss or graceful,
JEALOUSY in my crystal skull,
Jail a sea within that rips a soul,
GUILT in my crystal skull,
Gilt shame that permits to null,
LONELINESS in my crystal skull,
Lonely nest to languish or lull,
DEPRESSION in my crystal skull,
Depress in infliction that is sorrowful.

I am the crystal skull,
Thirteen souls afflict my skull,
Thirteen mimes that lift and cull,
My skull glows when the moon is mystical full,
And theirs glow green with orange eyes,
Faces of death with a spiritual core rise,
See through their eyes, through your eyes they greeted,
Beat it or be defeated.

Still 6

Sixteen rhymes on a dead man's chest still,
Still, fine lines from my mind's treasure chest still,
Still chests rest but I never rest still,
Still attest of the weight on my chest still,
Still, there's poem breath that wades and never sets still,
Still through known death, quotes wait and won't forever-rest still,
Still blessed even when a curse stands to arrest still,
Sixteen rhymes of a dead man's chest still,
Still a chest of steel, never rusted even when will's test still,
Still, they try to pierce my heart at will; evil abreast still,
Still will they never kill when my will is at best still,
Still with the steering wheel, God never rests still,
Still divine intervention if my mind gets still,
Still find lines flowing that my mind gets still,
Still I'm sowing, time and pride swells my chest still,
Sixteen rhymes from a dead man's chest still.

Treasure hunt

Assured treasure,
Sure when you're sure,
Cure when you're perturbed,
Disturbed when you're unsure,
Ensured though from the cross,
Cost of Calvary never lost,
Across time the span lasts,
Task that never left man last,
Path that leads to unburied treasure,
Measure that will never desert,
Dessert that we don't deserve,
Served through God's very word,
Blurred in the heart's of men,
Then again, Jesus lives again,
When we remember Him,
In our soul He dwells within,
In your heart is where the treasure is,
Lives in your chest with His promises,
Gives this grace better than gold that won't rust,
Just believe and in Him just trust.

¿

Last stand of a madman,
Damned plan in a bad land,
Sad sham they implanted,
Managed to damn it,
Planet they willed dead,
Spilled red while they killed men,
Still led into the quicksand,
Quick plans of their sick stand.

The raider

Their literary game that I raid,
With their aim at my ire aid,
My unwanted tirade,
They only race to my retire aid,
Murder with mire to my template of mood,
Stoned raider in this temple of doom,
Or a gun to my temple and boom,
To me the Earth is the moon,
Where they made it my tomb,
They refute but their feelings are moot,
They can't defuse or mute,
The raider to the root,
Ready to raid here so take cover,
The raider of the takeover.

Coming
October 1, 2022

PEACE 3

THE CHAPBOOK

Coming
October 13, 2022

BOOK NUMBER THIRTEEN[4]

THE CHAPBOOK

Coming
HALLOWEEN   2022

More poetic tales of terror!

MIKE McCLUSKEY'S

HALLOWEEN HORROR VOL. II

THE CHAPBOOK

Other Poem Books by **Mike McCluskey**

"Patience Is Life"
2003

"F.T.W."
2004

"The Morgue"
2004

"What If…"
2005

"Book Of Rhymes"
2010

"Wicked"
2011

"Patience Is Life"
"Collector's Edition"
2013

"Therapy"
2016

"Amerikan Nightmare:
Supposedly A Dream"
2017

"Raider Of The Lost Art"
2022

Mike McCluskey on

Blurb.com
Amazon.com
Barnesandnoble.com
Youtube.com